Pokémon

FIRST PARTNER

HANDBOOK

by Simcha Whitehill

SCHOLASTIC INC.

ISBN 978-1-338-18533-1

10 9 8 7 6 5 4 3 2 1   17 18 19 20 21

Printed in the U.S.A.   161

First printing 2017

Designed by Kay Petronio

CONTENTS

MEET
ASH AND HIS
FIRST FRIENDS!

It's exciting to meet new friends, but there's nothing like old friends. You know, the buddies who have stood by you through good times and bad, through amazing triumphs and terrible troubles—and even some pretty intense Team Rocket attacks.

Ash Ketchum knows that he couldn't have made it far on his quest without the help and support of all his Pokémon pals, especially the ones who believed in him from the beginning. When he first started on his journey, he made four special friends who truly shaped his battle style: Pikachu, Bulbasaur, Charmander, and Squirtle. Their bonds of friendship and trust have made Ash the Pokémon Trainer he is today.

How did Ash become friends with these four cool and courageous Pokémon? If you want to find out, read on . . .

PIKACHU

One Pokémon has traveled with Ash everywhere, through Kanto, Johto, Hoenn, Sinnoh, Unova, Kalos, and Alola—and in style! Pikachu refuses to ride in its Poké Ball, so it's right by Ash's side at every step of the way.

Pikachu may look cute and cuddly, but don't let its adorable red cheeks fool you—they are charged full of electricity. Pikachu is known for its shockingly powerful Electric-type attacks, like Thunderbolt and Electro Ball. Ash often calls on Pikachu during Gym battles and tournaments.

This little Pokémon has a strong sense of right and wrong—it's known for its willingness to stand up to bullies, and it will bravely fight for what's right. Pikachu is protective of its best friend, Ash, and it's always willing to help a Pokémon in need. Pikachu is confident, friendly, and fun. That's probably why it's one of the most beloved Pokémon in the world!

PIKACHU'S POKÉDEX STATS

PIKACHU
MOUSE POKÉMON

Imperial Height: **1'04"**
Imperial Weight: **13.2 lbs.**
Metric Height: **0.4 m**
Metric Weight: **6.0 kg**
Type: **ELECTRIC**

Pikachu naturally stores up electricity in its body, and it needs to discharge that energy on a regular basis to maintain good health. To take advantage of this, some have suggested creating a Pikachu-fueled power plant.

Forget beauty sleep; the Mouse Pokémon needs a good night's rest for sheer battle strength. Pikachu's red cheeks are filled with electric power that recharges while it rests. So if you spot a sleeping Pikachu in the forest, be sure to keep quiet. You don't want to wake it up—it's important Pikachu gets its shut-eye!

Pikachu often zap first, ask questions later. Their first response to seeing new things and even people can be a Thunderbolt. So don't be shocked if you get shocked when you meet a wild Pikachu!

COSPLAY PIKACHU

While traveling through Kalos, Ash and his friends stumbled upon the largest Pikachu habitat they'd ever seen! The estate belonged to Pikachu fanatic Frank, a director who dreams of making a movie about a place called Pikachuland.

When Frank met Ash's pal Pikachu, he insisted it play the lead role in the movie, and a star was born!

Here are some of the other Pikachu actors from the movie in their costumes—thus, the name Cosplay Pikachu.

PIKACHU, PHD

PIKACHU LIBRE

PIKACHU POP STAR

PIKACHU BELLE

PIKACHU ROCK STAR

13

THE DAY ASH MET PIKACHU

HOW DID ASH AND PIKACHU'S STORY BEGIN? READ ON TO FIND OUT!

Ash overslept the day he got to pick his first partner Pokémon out at Professor Oak's lab. Since he was the last to arrive, the traditional Kanto first partner Pokémon—Bulbasaur, Squirtle, and Charmander—had all been claimed by other new Trainers.

There was only one Pokémon left, but Professor Oak wasn't sure if it was a good idea to pair a new Trainer with a Pokémon that had been returned to him three times. The Pokémon in question? Pikachu!

Now I know what you're thinking: Pikachu is one of the coolest Pokémon ever. It's traveled everywhere with Ash as his best friend. And it's all true—Ash and Pikachu are inseparable, they've fought hundreds of battles together, and they have a special bond.

But friendships take time to build. No pair just instantly becomes best friends. Certainly not Pikachu and Ash. In fact, on day one, you could say Pikachu saw Ash as the enemy!

But Ash was determined to win over the picky Pikachu. Now that he was finally ten, Ash wasn't going to let anything stop him from becoming a Pokémon Trainer.

However, Ash soon discovered it wasn't easy training a Pokémon rebel. When he welcomed Pikachu with a big hug, the Mouse Pokémon zapped him. Then it refused to go into its Poké Ball.

As they headed into the woods to begin their journey, Ash pleaded with Pikachu to give him a chance, but it was no use. So Ash let Pikachu roam free, hoping to earn

its trust. However, Pikachu just climbed a nearby tree and laughed at Ash when he tried and failed to catch his first wild Pokémon, a Pidgey.

Ash chased after Pidgey. But without a Pokémon to help him battle, he was helpless—even against the Tiny Bird Pokémon. Pidgey used Gust and Sand Attack to leave Ash in the dust.

Ash was embarrassed, but his spirit didn't waver. He stepped up his offense, throwing rocks to catch another wild Pokémon.

Ash's aim was good, but his plan was off. When one rock hit its target, the Pokémon—a fierce Spearow— got angry and retaliated . . . against

Pikachu! The little Electric-type Pokémon zapped Spearow with a Thunderbolt, but that only made Spearow madder, and it called for backup. Soon the sky filled with attacking Spearow! They began pecking away at Pikachu. Ash grabbed his new Pokémon and made a run for it.

After a few yards, Ash and Pikachu's path ended abruptly . . . at a cliff! Ash and Pikachu had to jump off, straight into a waterfall. The pair floated downstream, away from danger. But soon they got hooked in fishing

wire. The angler was a girl named
Misty, and she was surprised to discover
Ash and Pikachu at the end of her line!

Misty quickly saw that Pikachu was hurt after
the Spearow attack. It needed to visit the Pokémon
Center. She pointed them in the right direction, and then
Ash borrowed her bike to escape the
Spearow!

Rain pelted down on Ash
and Pikachu as they
hurried along. Then
the bike slipped
in the mud, and
the boy and his
Pokémon fell off.
And the Spearow
just kept coming!
Ash had no choice
but to take a stand.
He begged the angry
Pokémon not to hurt Pikachu,
offering to fight them himself instead.

Pikachu was so touched by Ash's bravery, it had a
change of heart. It mustered all its strength, hopped
up on Ash's shoulder, and dove right into the flock of
Spearow, unleashing a powerful Thunderbolt.

Zap! The blast of the Electric-type attack was so strong
that all the Spearow retreated. Even Misty's bike got fried
to a crisp!

And so the die was cast: Ash and Pikachu bonded as

best friends, and that tie turned out to be unbreakable. From that day on, the Trainer and the little Mouse Pokémon became best friends. Together, they're up for any adventure!

TEN AWESOME PIKACHU FACTS

Pikachu loves to eat ketchup. It will pour it on anything, even a battle! It once used a bottle of ketchup to block a tough move, Cut, from Scyther.

Pikachu's Thunderbolt packs quite a punch in battle, and it's also super effective against bicycles! Pikachu has zapped Misty, May, and Dawn's two-wheelers to dust with its powerful Electric-type attacks.

 Pikachu has rhythm! In a heated battle with the Anistar City Gym Leader, Olympia, Pikachu tapped its tail to keep the beat—and keep track of time for Ash.

 No one gets rid of trouble and makes it double better than Pikachu! Using its incredible Thunderbolt, it's sent Team Rocket blasting off hundreds of times.

 They say friends are the family you choose. When Ash and Pikachu met a pack of Pikachu living together in the woods, Ash figured his pal would be better off with them. So Ash ran away, but Pikachu chased after him. Pikachu chose its best friend, Ash!

 When the going gets tough, Pikachu shows it's a team player. When a Team Rocket plan backfired, Pikachu ended up stranded in the woods . . . while tied to

Meowth! Instead of picking a fight, Pikachu got Meowth to work together to find their way out.

Ash and Pikachu are always ready to step up and help a Pokémon in need! When Team Rocket locked Professor Sycamore's pal Garchomp in a control collar, Pikachu used its Iron Tail to slash through the neck brace and free the giant Pokémon.

Pikachu has a soft spot for Misty's pal Togepi. In Ash and Misty's battle to see who could catch Totodile, Misty called on Togepi, because she knew Pikachu would never ever use an attack on its friend. When it comes to Togepi, Pikachu is a lover, not a fighter.

Pikachu can use its charm to help Ash out of awkward situations. When Ash spotted Axew in the woods, he immediately tried to catch it, not realizing it had a Trainer already—Iris. But instead of getting mad, Iris got distracted by adorable Pikachu and decided to join them on their journey!

Pikachu is known for its Electric-type moves, but it also draws power from its self-esteem. Even though Ash had the Thunderstone to help it evolve, Pikachu decided to be true to itself.

PIKACHU'S BIG BATTLES

ASH AND PIKACHU HAVE UNSTOPPABLE CHEMISTRY WHEN THEY COMPETE TOGETHER! HERE'S A FEW HIGHLIGHTS FROM SOME OF THEIR MOST UNFORGETTABLE BATTLES.

In the qualifying round of the Unova League, Ash had to face his rival, Trip. Trip called on Serperior, and Ash avoided choosing a Pokémon with a type advantage. Instead, he went for heart, choosing his best buddy, Pikachu. It's a pick that paid off, as Ash and Pikachu won the round with an incredible combination of Electro Ball and Iron Tail!

During Ash's rematch in Santalune City, Gym Leader Viola had Vivillon use Sleep Powder to lull Pikachu into a loss. Then Ash had Pikachu use a move that seemed shocking. Pikachu used Electro Ball on itself to break the sleepy spell. Reenergized, Pikachu bolted back into the battle—and won the round with a terrific Thunderbolt!

When Brandon had Regice trap Pikachu in an ice cube, it looked like this match was on ice! But Ash rallied Pikachu to use Thunderbolt to melt itself back into the battle. Pikachu helped Ash earn a Battle Frontier victory!

🔴 At the Mahogany Gym, Ash chose Pikachu as his second Pokémon. When Piloswine turned a pool of water into an ice rink, Gym Leader Pryce suggested they give up. But Pikachu skated its way to victory. Together with Pikachu, Ash earned the Glacier Badge!

🔴 When Ash and Pikachu faced Bug-type expert and Gym Leader Burgh, Leavanny trapped Pikachu in sticky string. To shake it off, Ash sent Pikachu diving straight into Leavanny's Leaf Storm. The sharp leaves cut right through the strings, and Pikachu was freed! Ash and Pikachu defeated Burgh and Leavanny with a powerful Electro Ball, and Ash claimed the Insect Badge, his third Gym badge in Unova!

🔴 Ash met Brock for the first time when he was a challenger at the Pewter City Gym. In their first match, Brock and Onix stopped short of knocking out Pikachu. So when Pikachu got the upper hand in their rematch, it stopped before knocking out Onix. Impressed with Ash's sportsmanship, Brock awarded him the Boulder Badge—and then decided to join Ash on his journey.

🔴 Ash was in town to challenge Gym Leader Erika of Celadon City, but he accidentally made a bad first impression by insulting her perfume. He should have kept his nose out of it! He even let Team Rocket dress him up as a little blond girl named Ashly. It was all going great . . . until Pikachu's Thunderbolt zapped his wig and revealed Ash's true identity!

🔴 When Ash went to challenge Mauville City Gym Leader Wattson to a battle, he and Pikachu first met Raikou. But Pikachu soon discovered that Raikou was really a robot! Eventually, Ash and Pikachu got the chance to battle Wattson and his real Electric-type Pokémon pals. Pikachu won all three rounds with a single attack. Ash was awarded the Dynamo Badge, but something seemed fishy. When Ash discovered that Pikachu was overcharged from battling the mechanical Raikou, he tried to return the badge. Impressed with his honesty, Wattson insisted he keep the Dynamo Badge.

In Cyllage City, Ash and Pikachu faced Grant and his tough Tyrunt. First, Pikachu combatted Tyrunt's incredible Draco Meteor using a move Ash created: Draco Meteor Climb, in which Pikachu jumps on the attack to ride it out. Then Pikachu used its tail like a baseball bat and swung at Tyrunt's Rock Tomb stones to lodge a rock right in Tyrunt's mouth! With Tyrunt tongue-tied, Pikachu won both the battle and the Cliff Badge.

When Team Rocket tried to steal a famous Pokémon actor, Zorua, they made quite a scene! Pikachu used a powerful Electro Ball and Thunderbolt to stop them, and the huge blast wasn't just for show—it also stopped the terrible trio from stealing Zorua! Pikachu's amazing attacks had an impact, both on- and offscreen!

MEET SQUIRTLE

SQUIRTLE

Ash and his pal Squirtle are unstoppable on the battlefield! Over their travels through Kanto, the Orange Islands, and Johto, the Trainer and this Water-type Pokémon formed a tight bond. Their teamwork is so strong, it's hard to believe that Squirtle's previous Trainer abandoned it. Squirtle is one special Pokémon!

When Ash's little Water-type Pokémon was the leader of the Squirtle Squad, it played it tough. But deep down inside, Squirtle is a big softy for its friends. Plus, Squirtle really rocks a pair of sunglasses!

SQUIRTLE'S POKÉDEX STATS

SQUIRTLE
TINY TURTLE POKÉMON

Imperial Height: **1'08"**
Imperial Weight: **19.8 lbs.**
Metric Height: **0.5 m**
Metric Weight: **9.0 kg**
Type: **WATER**

With its aerodynamic shape and grooved surface, Squirtle's shell helps it cut through the water very quickly and offers protection in battle.

The shell also helps Squirtle shoot water at foes. Using an attack called Hydro Pump, the Tiny Turtle Pokémon can spray water from its arm and leg holes. So if you're battling Squirtle, get ready to get wet! It can splash an opponent from every direction.

FROM ONE SQUAD TO ANOTHER

HOW DID ASH AND SQUIRTLE FIRST MEET? READ ON TO FIND OUT!

While traveling through the forest one day, Ash stepped on some soft ground that turned into a trap. He, Misty, Brock, and Pikachu tumbled into a giant sinkhole!

Five Squirtle wearing sunglasses surrounded the sinkhole, laughing. There was no mystery about the culprits in this case!

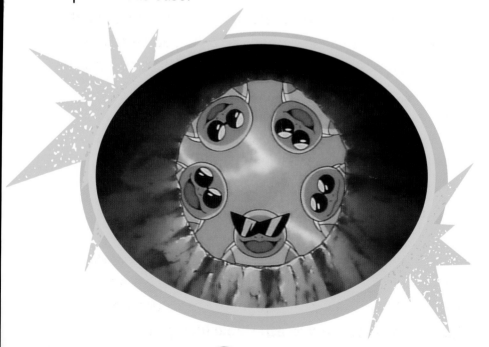

Pikachu zapped one Squirtle with Thunderbolt, and it looked like a battle was about to begin. But the sound of Officer Jenny's sirens in the distance soon scared away the Squirtle.

Officer Jenny rescued Ash and his friends and told them all about this band of mischievous bandits, who were known as the Squirtle Squad. The Squirtle often stole food, but Officer Jenny felt sorry for them—all five members of the squad had been abandoned by their Trainers.

Ash and his pals weren't the only ones who crossed paths with the Squirtle Squad that day. Their next victims? Team Rocket! The Squirtle Squad tied up Jessie, James, and Meowth and even stole their picnic basket.

Jessie tried to hire the squad for a special mission—catching Ash's pal Pikachu. At first, the Squirtle weren't interested. They didn't trust any humans after the way their Trainers had treated them.

But Meowth had an idea. He convinced the Squirtle Squad that he was really the leader of Team Rocket, and that Jessie and James were his pets! The Squirtle Squad set Meowth free and agreed to help him catch Pikachu.

A few hours later, while Ash and his friends were resting by a lake, the Squirtle

Squad launched a surprise attack!
Pikachu fired back with Thunderbolt, but
the squad leader was ready. It knocked Pikachu
into the lake. When Pikachu tried to swim back to
land, a Goldeen stabbed it with its horn. Pikachu was
really hurt!

The Squirtle Squad and their new friend Meowth
lassoed Ash, Brock, and Misty and brought everyone
back to their lair. Ash begged the Squirtle Squad to let
him get a Super Potion to heal Pikachu. When the squad
leader saw the tears in Ash's eyes, it agreed to let him go
get the medicine.

Ash reached the store after a tough trip through the forest. But then he discovered that Jessie and James had just robbed all the flash powder, promising to use it to bring an end to the Squirtle Squad.

Ash and Officer Jenny raced back to their friends just in time to find Team Rocket dropping flash powder bombs out of their hot air balloon! Meowth grabbed Pikachu and hopped on Team Rocket's ride.

The Squirtle Squad, Ash, Misty, and Brock hurried inside the shelter of the cave. But the squad's leader fell on its back and couldn't get up. Ash ran to the Squirtle and shielded it with his body. Then Ash told Squirtle to run to safety. But instead, Squirtle lifted Ash above its head and carried *him* to safety!

Squirtle used Water Gun to poke a big hole in Team Rocket's balloon. Pikachu fell out of the basket, and Ash dived to catch his pal. They were all safe!

Before anyone could celebrate, Officer Jenny spotted a fire in the woods. The whole Squirtle Squad fired Water Gun at the blaze. Working together, the squad and their new friends put out a terrible forest fire. The Squirtle

Squad's strength and teamwork saved the day and the town!

Officer Jenny presented the Squirtle Squad with cool uniforms and an even cooler appointment—official town firefighters!

Ash, Misty, Brock, and Pikachu were ready to begin the next leg of their journey. But this happy ending brought a new beginning: Squirtle asked to join Ash. Ash proved that he was a caring Trainer, and Squirtle was eager to join his team!

SUPERB SQUIRTLE STATS

Stylish Squirtle is known for sporting a cool pair of sunglasses from time to time. When Ash first met Squirtle, it was easy to pick out from its pack because of its unique choice in eyewear.

Squirtle isn't afraid to stand up to anyone or anything. When it failed to put out the fuse on Team Rocket's dynamite, it kept on digging out its beloved Trainer, Ash, from beneath the rubble.

 Squirtle's Water Gun can save the day in so many ways! It can win a heated battle, and it can also put out a fierce fire. When the Celadon Gym and all its perfume went up in flames, Squirtle used Water Gun to fight the fire.

Squirtle is not just a cool Pokémon pal, it can also be a fun ride! Pikachu had the chance to surf on Squirtle's shell as it crossed the lake in a Pokémon race.

Squirtle can spray evil away. Its Water-type moves are so strong, they can act like a hose and send Team Rocket flying!

 Paparazzi, beware! Squirtle won't let anyone snap a photo of Ash without his permission. To get photographer Todd Snap out of the bushes, Ash called on Squirtle to fire its Water Gun. After Todd washed up, he and Ash eventually became pals.

 Before the fifth round of the Indigo Conference, Team Rocket kidnapped Ash and Pikachu and threw them in the back of their big truck. Determined to escape, Ash asked Squirtle to flood the truck with Water Gun. It was no small task, but Squirtle made it happen! With water bursting out the sides, the truck slid off the road, and Ash and his Pokémon pals were free!

 Squirtle likes to keep the heat on the battlefield and out of its meals. The Tiny Turtle Pokémon can't stand spicy food. When Squirtle accidentally ate some hot stuff at a party in Pallet Town, it was unable to fire its famous Water Gun. So Misty asked her buddy Staryu to put out the fire inside Squirtle's mouth!

 Squirtle is such a nice Pokémon, it once helped Team Rocket! Ash was honored to carry the Indigo League torch, fired up by the Legendary Pokémon Moltres's flame. But then Team Rocket surprised Ash and snatched it. Jessie, James, and Meowth were so careless with the torch that Meowth and Victreebel accidentally caught fire. So Ash asked Squirtle to put out the flames with Water Gun. Their good deed didn't stop Team Rocket from carrying out their dastardly plan, but Ash and Squirtle always do what's right—and that's why they always prevail in the end.

 Squirtle is a natural leader who earns the respect of other Pokémon. When Ash first met Squirtle, it was the head of a tough pack of Pokémon abandoned by their Trainers known as the Squirtle Squad.

FIRING UP THE SQUIRTLE FIRE SQUAD

Ash loves a good competition! So he couldn't resist entering the Johto Fire and Rescue Grand Prix. But there was one big problem—he didn't have enough Water-type Pokémon on his team. So he decided to borrow Misty's Pokémon pals Psyduck and Staryu, and he chose Pikachu and Squirtle to create his ultimate team.

The competition was stiff. Teams of Golduck, Marill, Quagsire, and even the winners of the previous year's grand prix, Captain Aiden and Team Wartortle, all entered the contest. Ash and Squirtle had met Aiden and his team back on the Orange Islands, where Squirtle helped the Wartortle firefighters put out a raging local fire.

Next, Office Jenny and the Squirtle Squad arrived. Ash's Squirtle couldn't believe its eyes. It ran over to high-tail its pals. (That's slapping a high five, if you're a member of the Squirtle Squad!)

All the friends decided to train for the competition together. But the Squirtle Squad seemed really nervous. At target practice, Wartortle hit every mark, while the Squirtle Squad couldn't seem to hit one. Ash's Squirtle

returned to its friends to act as their leader again. Under their former leader's direction, the squad got back in the game.

When the time for the big competition came, Ash's Squirtle, Pikachu, Staryu, and Psyduck were up against Team Muk to put out a fake house fire. Staryu was so excited, it accidentally fired right at Psyduck, throwing it into the blaze. Squirtle hurried to save its pal. Team Ash tried their best, but they were no match for Team Muk, who smothered the blaze in seconds.

Next up, Officer Jenny and the Squirtle Squad began competing against the previous year's second-place winners, Team Golduck. The Golduck snapped into

action, but the Squirtle Squad was scared and didn't know what to do. They needed their leader!

Squirtle boldly stepped up to instruct its friends. Together as a team, they put out the blaze and won the round in no time.

But before the Squirtle Squad could celebrate, Team Rocket set a new fire on the field! Their evil robot blasted blazes out of its arms. Ash rallied Squirtle, who sprang into action and had the squad fire Water Gun. The other Water-type Pokémon jumped in to help, too, but Team Rocket scooped them all up in a net.

Jessie, James, and Meowth
captured every single Pokémon except
the Squirtle Squad, who were still ready to fight.
Squirtle instructed its pals to fire at the robot's belly
until it finally fell over. Timberrrrrr!

The Squirtle Squad hopped inside the head of the beast, stomping around and splashing the controls with water until all the Pokémon friends were free. The entire arena audience celebrated the Squirtle Squad's incredible victory.

As Ash watched Squirtle return to its role as the leader of the squad, he realized it belonged back together with its team. All the Squirtle in the squad agreed: They needed their friend, especially because they were about to compete in the final round.

In the finals, the Squirtle Squad faced Aiden and Team Wartortle, the evolved form of Squirtle. With Squirtle's guidance, the squad put out the big blaze seconds before Team Wartortle to cinch the win. Squirtle was super proud of the squad's victory, and it was absolutely overjoyed to be back with its old pals.

Now for the hard part: Squirtle had to say good-bye to its new friends, Ash, Bulbasaur, and Pikachu. But Ash reminded his beloved Squirtle that they would always be friends, no matter what.

Squirtle couldn't agree more. It rode away with Officer Jenny and its old pals, thrilled to be in back in charge of the newly decorated Squirtle Fire Squad.

FIVE SPLASHY SQUIRTLE MOMENTS

HERE ARE A FEW MORE OF SQUIRTLE'S MARVELOUS MOMENTS!

When Team Rocket stole Eevee and tried to evolve it into something evil, Squirtle stepped up to stop them! With one incredible blast of its super-strong Water Gun, Team Rocket and their plot were washed up.

When Dodrio got its necks tied in a knot, it went berserk. Dr. Proctor tried to help, but it was no use. So Ash called on fearless Squirtle to use Water Gun to knock out the anxious Pokémon so it could receive the treatment it needed.

In the second battle of the Indigo Conference, Ash chose Squirtle as his final Pokémon. And it was the perfect pick! Squirtle wowed the audience with a Water Gun and Skull Bash combo so strong, it won the round against Nidorino.

In a Water Gun challenge against the Mikan Gym Leader and Seadra, Ash called on Squirtle to show off its aim. In the first round, Squirtle knocked over cans with

its precise Water Gun. In the second
challenge, Squirtle shot right through clay
pigeons as they sped through the sky. Squirtle really
made a splash in this competition!

In the final round of Ash's Trovita Island Gym battle
with Rudy, Starmie showed it could use Electric moves,
and it looked like Ash didn't have a chance. But Squirtle
surprised everyone with a new trick up its sleeve—Hydro
Pump. With its amazing new attack,
it knocked out its opponent and
helped Ash win the Spike
Shell Badge!

MEET BULBASAUR

BULBASAUR

Brave Bulbasaur isn't the kind of Pokémon you can push around. It always has its friends' backs, too. This tiny Grass- and Poison-type will stand up to bullies, and it uses its strong vines to whip any situation.

Bulbasaur's stubbornness and desire to fight for what's right are precisely why it was the perfect Pokémon to join Ash on his journey. Together, they traveled through Kanto, the Orange Islands, Johto, and Hoenn.

BULBASAUR'S POKÉDEX STATS

BULBASAUR
SEED POKÉMON

Imperial Height: **2'04"**
Imperial Weight: **15.2 lbs.**
Metric Height: **0.7 m**
Metric Weight: **6.9 kg**
Type: **GRASS-POISON**

Carrying the weight of the bud on its back makes Bulbasaur's legs stronger. When the bud is close to blooming, the Pokémon spends more time sleeping in the sun.

While it might seem hard to sleep in all that light, that's the bright spot for Bulbasaur. As the rays beam down on its bulb, its bulb grows—and so does its energy.

BEFRIENDING BULBASAUR

On their way to Vermilion City, Ash, Brock, and Misty found themselves lost in the forest. But they did find a wild Oddish. Both Trainers wanted to catch the Pokémon, but Misty beat Ash to the battle. She called on Staryu to spray Water Gun and use Tackle, but before she could throw her Poké Ball, a tough Bulbasaur stepped up to protect Oddish.

Ash was excited—he wanted to try to catch the wild Bulbasaur. He chose Butterfree and asked it to spray Sleep Powder. Bulbasaur blew a strong wind to send the Sleep Powder back at Butterfree. Then Bulbasaur and Oddish made their escape, heading back into the woods.

Ash and his friends decided to try to search for the Pokémon. But the woods were riddled with traps!

A rope bridge broke, and Brock slipped off into a river. Misty tumbled into a dangerous sinkhole, and then Ash and Misty got caught in a net.

Luckily, Brock was able to set his friends free. Then he told them about an incredible girl named Melanie who ran a special Hidden Village for Pokémon. She was the one who set all those traps—to protect her Pokémon friends from getting caught by Trainers.

Brock took Ash and Misty to Melanie's cabin, which was surrounded by Pokémon who'd come to rest and relax. Melanie told the Trainers it was a Pokémon health spa dedicated to helping Pokémon who need to heal from injury, or who've been abandoned by their Trainers. The wild Oddish was left alone in the woods by a Trainer who thought it was too weak.

Once she heard its story, Misty was sorry for battling Oddish. With tears in her eyes, she apologized to Oddish. The little Pokémon was so touched, it wiped away her tears.

Suddenly, Bulbasaur ran up and tackled Misty, thinking she was on the attack again. Ash was determined to get a rematch, but Melanie stopped him. She explained that Bulbasaur protected the Pokémon at her village and it was just looking out for Oddish. Ash immediately backed down, but Bulbasaur was still snarling.

Suddenly, Team Rocket swooped in! Jessie, James, and Meowth landed right beside the cabin and unleashed a huge vacuum to suck up all the Pokémon in the village.

Brock, Misty, Ash, and Melanie rushed all the Pokémon back inside the cabin. But one Pokémon went flying— Oddish. Bulbasaur used its vines to reel Oddish in. Then Ash helped hold down Oddish and Bulbasaur as they all struggled against the pull of the giant vacuum.

Finally, everyone was safely back in the cabin. But Team Rocket wasn't done. They turned the vacuum on the cabin itself!

Bulbasaur hopped up on the roof and slapped away the sucker with Vine Whip. Ash had Pidgeotto use Gust to counter the vacuum suck. The combination of moves turned the air push and pull into a tornado! Team Rocket and their vacuum were sent blasting off in the gale.

Impressed by their teamwork, Melanie asked Ash if he would take Bulbasaur along on his journey. Ash was thrilled, though he couldn't help worrying about taking away the spa's Pokémon protector. But Melanie said Bulbasaur deserved the chance to see the world.

Bulbasaur wanted to join Ash, too, but first it demanded a rematch. Ash chose Pikachu, but before it could spring into action, Bulbasaur got its vines wrapped around the Mouse Pokémon. Pikachu sent a jolt of electricity down its vines. Swiftly, Ash threw his Poké Ball and caught his brave new pal!

Pikachu's battle strategy worked. Bulbasaur officially became part of the team!

BULBASAUR IN BATTLE

WANT TO DISCOVER SOME OF BULBASAUR'S BIGGEST BATTLES? READ ON!

At a practice battle in the woods, Ash chose Bulbasaur to battle Rhyhorn. But Rhyhorn's tough Take Down nearly knocked Bulbasaur out! Ash tried to get Bulbasaur to return to its Poké Ball, but it refused. With a shot of its amazing Razor Leaf, Bulbasaur wound up winning the round against Rhyhorn.

When Ash battled Ninja Warrior Aya at the Fuchsia City Gym, he called on his buddy Bulbasaur to take on Venonat. Bulbasaur got confused in Venonat's strong Psybeam, but it focused and added its draining Leech Seed. Ash was proud of their victory, but to earn the Soul Badge, he'd have to battle Aya's older brother, the Gym Leader Koga.

 In the tournament for Togepi, Ash battled Misty for the first time since the Cerulean City Gym. Psyduck surprised Misty by choosing itself for the battle against Bulbasaur. Ash's battle style was usually untraditional, but even so, this match was super silly! Ash told Bulbasaur to lick Psyduck's head and then use Tickle. Bulbasaur ended up giggling its way to the round win!

When Misty wanted to enter the Queen Princess Festival, Ash, Brock, and their Pokémon offered to help. Ash's buddy Bulbasaur impressed everyone by winning its round with Kingler in one incredible move—Vine Whip.

 At the Indigo Conference, Ash called on Bulbasaur to battle Jeanette and Beedrill. Surprisingly, Ash picked his Pokémon pal with the type advantage in a battle on a grassy field. It's not his style to be so sensible, but the strategy worked. Although Beedrill had a superb Poison Sting, Bulbasaur won the round with a combination of an energy-sapping Leech Seed and a hard-hitting Tackle . . .

 . . . but the Indigo Conference wasn't over, and Bulbasaur was still in top form! Its next opponent was

one strong Scyther. Buddies Ash and
Bulbasaur had a smart team strategy.
When Scyther surrounded Bulbasaur with
Double Team, Bulbasaur sliced right through the
fakes with Vine Whip.

 When Ash battled Trovita Island Gym Leader Rudy,
he chose Bulbasaur for the Grass-type battle against
Exeggutor. Bulbasaur sent all three of Exeggutor's heads
to naptime with its super-strong Sleep Powder.

 When Misty and Ash both wanted to train Totodile, they decided to settle the argument with a battle. Ash called on Bulbasaur for a match against Poliwag. The battle got so heated, Poliwag evolved into Poliwhirl. Just when it looked like Misty and her newly evolved pal had sealed the win, Bulbasaur blasted a big Solar Beam. With that unbelievably bright attack, Ash and Bulbasaur won the round, and their new friend Totodile joined them on their journey!

At the H division of the Johto Conference, Ash was up against Jackson and Meganium from New Bark Town. The scene was so tense, Bulbasaur and Meganium started fighting before the round even started! Once the battle began, Meganium used Razor Leaf; Bulbasaur used Razor Leaf. Bulbasaur used Vine Whip; Meganium used Vine Whip. This battle of sheer strength ended in a double knockout and a draw. However, both Bulbasaur and Meganium did win something—respect for each other.

FIVE FUN FACTS ABOUT BULBASAUR

HERE'S SOME TERRIFIC TRIVIA ABOUT THIS SUN-LOVING, FUN-LOVING POKÉMON!

Bulbasaur might love to battle, but it also knows how to keep the peace. When Professor Oak's laboratory garden, a haven for wild Pokémon, turned into a battleground, he called on Ash and his wise Bulbasaur to break up the fight. Bulbasaur fired up such a bright Solar Beam that all the angry Pokémon finally saw the light. Basking in Solar Beam's rays, they all relaxed, and peace was restored. Just call it Ambassador Bulbasaur!

Bulbasaur is an excellent builder. When Professor Oak wanted to construct another lake at his lab, Bulbasaur rallied the local Pokémon and turned them into a construction crew. Whether the building challenge was bedrock or boulders, Bulbasaur the contractor was a Pokémon with a plan!

 When a fire onboard a shipwreck trapped Ash and his friends, Ash asked his pal Bulbasaur to extend its Vine Whip over the fire. Thanks to Bulbasaur, everyone was able to cross to safety!

 To win the Sea Ruby Badge, Gym Leader Danny puts Trainers to the test. First Bulbasaur used its vines to steer Ash's sled. That made their sled go awry—and then Team Rocket showed up to ruin their race! When Ash, Danny, and their Pokémon pals fell into Team Rocket's snow trap, Bulbasaur's vines helped Ash and his friends climb out and rescue Pikachu.

 Bulbasaur is not food, but just try telling Ash's pal Heracross that! Heracross is always trying to steal some sweet sap from its bulb.

MEET CHARMANDER

CHARMANDER

If you wanted to describe Ash's little Lizard Pokémon pal in one word, that would have to be loyal. Charmander seemed to outgrow that description when it evolved into Charmeleon and Charizard. This Fire-type Pokémon sure is hotheaded! It wouldn't listen to its Trainer, and it would only battle Pokémon that earned its respect. But Charmeleon and Charizard were so strong, their matches were always red-hot!

No matter what his Fire-type friend chose to do, Ash always supported and cared about Charmander. They've parted ways and reunited a few times, but they've always remained devoted to each other. Together, they've traveled though parts of Kanto, the Orange Islands, Johto, Unova and the Decolore Islands.

CHARMANDERS'S POKÉDEX STATS

CHARMANDER
LIZARD POKÉMON

Imperial Height: **2'00"**
Imperial Weight: **18.7 lbs.**
Metric Height: **0.6 m**
Metric Weight: **8.5 kg**
Type: **FIRE**

The flame on Charmander's tail tip indicates how the Pokémon is feeling. It flares up in a fury when Charmander is angry!

If the flame looks a little dim, Charmander isn't feeling up to snuff and needs to be taken to the Pokémon Center. But when the fire blazes up, this Pokémon is ready to battle.

A SECOND CHANCE FOR CHARMANDER

HOW DID ASH AND CHARMANDER FIRST MEET? READ ON TO FIND OUT!

When Ash, Misty, Brock, and Pikachu got lost on their way to Vermilion City, they stumbled across a giant Pokémon. Pikachu tried to hide, but as the friends drew closer, they realized the enormous-seeming Pokémon was actually a little Charmander, perched on top of a giant rock.

Ash was excited. He told his pals that Charmander was his first pick for first partner Pokémon, but he missed his chance to choose it at Professor Oak's lab. Now he couldn't wait to catch the little Fire-type.

But before Ash began battling, Brock noticed that Charmander looked pretty weak. He suggested Ash should catch it in a Poké Ball and take it to rest at the Pokémon Center. Ash agreed, and tossed his Poké Ball at the Lizard Pokémon.

But suddenly, Charmander jumped up and swatted the ball with its tail.

Charmander sure didn't look weak after a move like that, but Ash tried again. Direct hit!

The Poké Ball blinked, but Charmander popped back out and whacked the ball right at Ash's head!

Pikachu tried talking to Charmander. The little Fire-type said it was waiting for its Trainer to come back. So Ash decided to continue down the road with his crew.

But when the friends reached the local Pokémon Center, it started raining. Brock worried about Charmander. Its flame was already weak, and this weather could put it out.

A bunch of Trainers had gathered at the Pokémon Center to wait out the storm. Ash, Brock, and Misty overheard one bragging about how he'd just abandoned a weak Charmander. The Trainer, Damian, claimed Charmander was so dumb it wouldn't stop following him. So Damian left it on a rock and promised to come back, and Charmander believed him.

Brock, Misty, and Ash were certain Damian was talking about the Charmander they'd just passed in the woods. Brock was furious. He told Damian that Charmander was still waiting for him, and demanded that Damian get it out of the rain. But Damian wasn't

interested in saving Charmander—
only in battling Ash, Misty, and Brock!

Nurse Joy broke up the fight, and Damian walked away, but he was still set on walking out on Charmander.

So, Brock, Ash, and Misty came to the rescue. They headed out through the pouring rain to find the Fire-type Pokémon. It was still perched on that same rock, using a leaf as an umbrella. Worse yet, a few Spearow had started pecking at it. Ash threw a rock to scare the Spearow away, and Pikachu fired Thunder Shock.

Charmander was clearly hurting. The flame on its tail was so small, it was nearly out. Ash, Brock, and Misty rushed it back to the Pokémon Center.

The next morning, Brock went to check on Charmander—and discovered it had run away! Ash was

certain it had gone back to that rock
to wait for its Trainer.

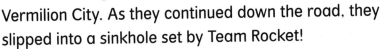

Ash was worried, but Nurse
Joy said there was no way
to protect Charmander from
its Trainer until it realized the
truth about him.

So, Ash, Misty, and Brock
decided to forge on to
Vermilion City. As they continued down the road, they
slipped into a sinkhole set by Team Rocket!

Charmander heard Pikachu's cries and rushed over
to help. It fired a fierce flame at Team Rocket, blasting
them off. Ash and his pals were all free! Ash was so
grateful to Charmander, he asked whether it would like
to join them on their journey. But then Damian appeared.
He'd witnessed the whole scene and was impressed
that Charmander scared off Team Rocket, and now that
Charmander was strong, he wanted it back.

But Charmander whacked Damian's Poké Ball
back with its tail. Angry, Damian threatened to crush
Charmander in battle. But before he could choose a
Pokémon to face the little Fire-type, Charmander aimed
a fiery blaze at him. Pikachu jumped in for support and
electrified the fire. Together, they made sure Damian
wouldn't ever bother Charmander again.

Ash asked Charmander one last time if it would like
to join him and his Pokémon friends, and this time,
Charmander accepted! It was so thrilled, it jumped into
the Poké Ball, ready to start over with its new pal.

ALL ABOUT CHARMANDER

Charmander lights up a room—and sometimes even a cave! The flame on the end of its tail isn't just awesome in battle, it also makes an awesome torch.

Even when it was small, two-foot-tall Charmander wasn't afraid of anything or anyone . . . except ghosts. When a Pokémon Tower in Lavender Town appeared haunted, Charmander and Ash's Pokémon pals raced out in terror. Fortunately, it turned out to be Gengar, Gastly, and Haunter, Ghost-Poison-type Pokémon with playful senses of humor.

Charmander trained with Ash for so long that it evolved into Charmeleon, and finally into Charizard. The only thing stronger than Charizard's attacks is its ego. When Ash can't seem to motivate it, competition can. If Charizard is impressed by a Pokémon's power, it relishes the fight.

When Ash tried to introduce Charizard to Tracey Sketchit's powerful Scyther, it couldn't even be bothered to say hello. But when it saw Scyther's show of strength against Team Rocket, Charizard jumped in to battle the trio.

When Ash passed through a festival about his home region, Kanto, he realized how much he missed his old Pokémon pal Charizard. So he called Professor Oak and asked him to send over his friend. It felt good for Trainer and Pokémon to be together again!

When they reunited in Unova, Charizard was happy to see Ash. But he was less happy to meet Iris's Pokémon pal, Dragonite. The two immediately became rivals. Finally, Ash decided to turn their sparks into a full-on battle. But once the two Pokémon were face to face in a fight, they earned a mutual respect for each other's power and courage. Later, they united as a team to help Clair find her missing Dragonite.

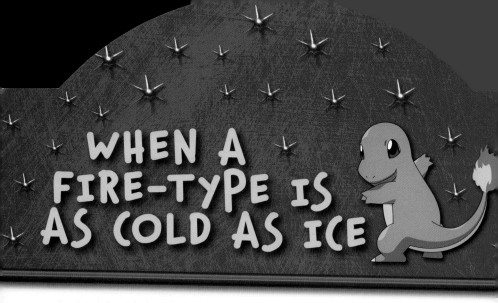

WHEN A FIRE-TYPE IS AS COLD AS ICE

While Misty, Tracey, Ash, and Pikachu were riding through the ocean on Lapras, they swam by a Trainer named Tad. He offered them a ride on his boat because he'd heard all about Ash's last battle. Then he challenged Ash to a battle. Always ready for fun, Ash accepted Tad's challenge, so Tad docked his boat on a nearby island.

At first, Ash chose Pikachu to battle Tad's Poliwrath. But he soon realized Pikachu was in over its head. To win this battle, Ash was going to have to fire things up.

So Ash chose Charizard. Ever since it evolved, Charizard had been pretty rude to its Trainer. And sure enough, as it entered the battlefield, it shot flames at Ash, and then flew into the sky to avoid him.

Confused, Tad asked Ash if he really wanted to choose

Charizard. But Ash was determined to stand by his Pokémon pick. So Tad instructed Poliwrath to fire Water Gun at the flying Charizard.

The attack grounded Charizard, and it landed proudly, facing Poliwrath. Ash asked if it was ready to battle. Charizard turned back to look at its Trainer with cold eyes, then whacked him with its tail.

Charizard bathed Poliwrath in flames, but to no effect. Ash pleaded with Charizard to work together as a team, with a strategy. But Charizard ignored him and fired flames at Poliwrath again and again. Poliwrath responded with Water Gun, and Charizard tried to

dodge, but the Water-type attack splashed the flame on its tail. Poliwrath quickly added another attack—a freezing Ice Beam.

Charizard fell to the ground, trapped inside an ice cube. Ash rushed over and tried to break it free with a rock, Tad returned Poliwrath to its Poké Ball and offered Ash a rematch.

Ash and his friends scrambled to build a fire. Charizard was free from the ice, but it was still freezing and too tired to stay awake. Ash rubbed its back, trying to warm it up. His hands turned red and raw from the hard work, but Ash didn't care.

Ash nursed Charizard through the night. He admitted he might not be the best Trainer in the world. He said he knew he'd made mistakes, but that he was trying to get better. Ash confided that his dream was to battle with Charizard side by side, as a team.

Charizard was touched by Ash's honesty. Its mind filled with happy memories of the time they'd shared.

When Charizard woke the next morning, it had

completely regained its strength.

But before it could reconnect with Ash, there was a rumble underfoot. A Team Rocket robot emerged from underground! Jessie, James, and Meowth captured Pikachu and tried to make a quick escape by digging back through the ground.

Ash raced after them. To his surprise, Charizard swooped in and offered him a ride. Then the Flame Pokémon jumped on Team Rocket's machine and prepared to cover it in a blaze. Ash begged Charizard not to use a fire attack, because Pikachu was still trapped in the robot. Instead, he asked Charizard to stomp on the robot and break its cage. Amazingly, Charizard listened and did exactly what Ash asked. And it worked! Pikachu was freed.

But Team Rocket wasn't about to roll over. They tried to attack Charizard with a spinning saw. When it dodged the blade, Pikachu and Ash were accidentally thrown to the ground. Charizard was so angry it powered up a fierce Rage fireball and sent Team Rocket blasting off.

Ash was so proud and so happy to be a team again. Tracey, Misty, and Tad hurried over to congratulate Ash and Charizard. It looked like Charizard's most powerful weapon just might just be its heart.

CHARMANDER'S BIG BATTLES

When Bulbasaur and Squirtle tried and failed to catch a very rambunctious wild Primeape, only Charmander was up for the challenge! It used its special move, Rage, which strengthens the more Charmander is under attack. With that kind of amazing strength, Charmander's flame grew and it was able to finally overpower Primeape!

In the first round of Ash's battle for the Rainbow Badge in Celadon City, Ash called on Charmander to battle Gym Leader Erika and Weepinbell. The town is known for perfume, and Charmander experienced the sweet smell of success when its fierce Flamethrower won the match.

When Ash finally got the chance to battle Gym Leader Koga in Fuchsia City, Team Rocket interrupted the match. Once they were sent blasting off, Charmander took to the battlefield and won a round against Golbat by using flashy Fire Spin. Ash was awarded the Soul Badge!

On the battlefield, Charmander is on fire, and so are its attacks! During a heated match with Ash and Charmander, the leader of the Bridge Bike Gang returned his pal Golem, but Charmander's attacks were so fiery, it made Golem's Poké Ball hot enough to burn the leader's hands!

When Charizard refused to battle during a match with Rhydon and Cinnabar Gym Leader Blaine on a battlefield atop a volcano, Ash was embarrassed. So imagine Ash's surprise when Charizard couldn't resist battling Blaine's Magmar, who stepped out of the hot lava of the volcano and directly onto the battlefield!

During Ash's rematch with Blaine, Magmar pushed Charizard into the volcano. Ash was worried about Charizard drowning in the hot lava, but it soared straight up into the sky with Magmar on its back! Thanks to Charizard, Ash won the Volcano Badge!

At the Indigo Conference, Ash had only one Pokémon pick left to beat Richie and his tough Pokémon pal, a Charmander named Zippo. Ash took a chance and chose Charizard. To Ash's surprise, his picky pal agreed to battle, and won the match! But the round wasn't over yet . . .

. . . when Charizard faced its next opponent, a little Pikachu named Sparky, it decided to take a nap on the field and forfeit the round!

In the Double Battle with Orange Crew Gym Leader Luana at the Kumquat Gym, Ash called on Pikachu and Charizard to take on Alakazam and Marowak. At first, Pikachu and Charizard seemed more interested in fighting

each other. As the battle wore on,
Charizard took on both opponents and got
trapped in Alakazam's Psychic attack. Ash begged
Pikachu to step in, and it used a powerful Thunder Shock
to free Charizard. Touched by Pikachu's help, Charizard
changed its tune, and the two began battling as a team.
Together, they earned Ash the Jade Star Badge!

At the Orange League Championship, Charizard and
Ash faced off against undefeated Trainer Drake and his
buddy, the impressive Electabuzz. They won a round with
Charizard's strong Seismic Toss.

Charizard is so big and strong, some Pokémon don't
stand a chance. When Casey chose Pidgey to battle the
Flame Pokémon, the Tiny Bird Pokémon was knocked out
by a single puff of its breath from its snout . . .

⬤ . . . and the next Pokémon Casey chose didn't fare any better. Casey called on Rattata, but it was knocked out by its own first attack! When it rammed into Charizard with Tackle, it wound up being the one to take the hit.

⬤ When Ash and his rival Gary Oak went head to head in the Johto Silver Conference, Ash chose Charizard as his final Pokémon. Gary, on the other hand, had three Pokémon picks left. The fate of the entire round rested on the Flame Pokémon's shoulders. Using a fierce Flamethrower, Charizard prevailed in its match with Scizor. Two more challengers to go . . .

⬤ . . . with an incredible Dragon Rage, Charizard rolled Golem out of the next match . . .

⬤ . . . and in the final matchup, Gary chose Blastoise. When its Flamethrower had no effect on Blastoise, Ash had Charizard cover the field with Flamethrower. When Blastoise tried cooling it off with Hydro Pump, the field was covered in a thick fog. Charizard sneaked up on Blastoise, and soon they were locked in close combat. Blastoise couldn't hit it with Hydro Pump, and now

Charizard could carry it high up into the sky for an epic Seismic Toss. With that incredible drop, Charizard won the round—and Ash defeated his rival Gary.

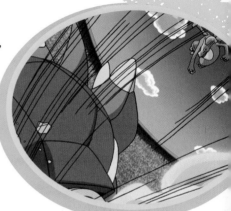

When Dragonite went on a rampage, searing its hometown, no one could stop it—except Charizard. It swooped in to save Ash and Pikachu, and then it stood up to the confused and fiery Dragon-Flying-type.

With one more badge left to qualify for the Johto Silver Conference, Ash called on his pal Charizard to battle Clair and Dragonair. Although it might have been a fairer fight on land, Dragonair had the advantage, since the battle took place in a pool of water. When Charizard pulled off its incredibly powerful Seismic Toss, it won the round—and Ash earned the Rising Badge!

THE REUNION RUMBLE

When Ash got the chance for a rematch with Frontier Brain Brandon, he knew he needed to get his first friends back together! Professor Oak brought Bulbasaur, who had been busy watching over all the Pokémon at his lab. Officer Jenny rode up with Squirtle, who had been putting out fires with its Squirtle Fire Squad. Charizard swooped down from the sky to give Ash a big hug.

Ash had planned a cool camping trip in the woods so his friends could hang out and get some training in. The Pokémon pals sat around the campfire while Ash reminisced, telling the stories of how he first met them all.

The next day, Ash, Squirtle, Bulbasaur, Pikachu, and Charizard got back to training. Seeing one another's strengths made them respect the amazing Pokémon team they'd become. But they weren't the only ones who were impressed.

Brandon, the Pyramid King, was in awe. He announced that he was ready to accept Ash's rematch challenge! The match was set to be four-on-four, and Pikachu, Charizard, Bulbasaur, and Squirtle couldn't wait to face Brandon together.

The Battle Pyramid was brimming with excitement. Many of Ash's friends and even Professor Oak had come to root for him. Before Ash took the field, the owner of the Battle Frontier, Scott, wished him luck and told him that if he won, he'd become a Frontier Brain himself!

As the sun beat down on the battlefield, Ash called on Charizard! Brandon chose Dusclops, a Ghost-type Pokémon. It was an even-type match and a seemingly even-strength match as Dusclops's Will-O-Wisp and Charizard's Flamethrower canceled each other out in midair.

This battle would be all about strategy! Brandon asked Dusclops to use Mean Look to stop Charizard from returning. As Charizard was pounded with a couple of powerful Shadow Punches, it became unable to battle.

Brandon won the first match, but the battle wasn't over yet! Next, Ash chose Bulbasaur. Again, Dusclops used Mean Look and kept Bulbasaur from being able to return.

Bulbasaur responded by wrapping Dusclops in a trap—its incredibly energy-draining Leech Seed. Dusclops was starting to look tired. But when it added Confusion, Bulbasaur got so mixed up, it started attacking itself with Vine Whip!

Ash reminded Bulbasaur that he'd always be there to help his friend, and his words helped Bulbasaur cut out the Confusion. Dusclops tried to hit it with a bold Will-O-Wisp, but Bulbasaur sent over a Solar Beam so strong, Dusclops was unable to battle. Bulbasaur won the match!

When Brandon chose Bug-and-Flying-type Ninjask, Ash switched out Bulbasaur and brought in Squirtle. Squirtle used its amazing wall of water, while Ninjask used a clever combination of Sandstorm and Sand Attack to blow dirt in Squirtle's eyes. Since it couldn't see, Ash advised Squirtle to rely on another sense—hearing. Ninjask came in for an Aerial Ace swoop, and at just the right moment, Squirtle released a wash of Hydro Pump. Ninjask's Aerial Ace cut through the wall of water, rinsing Squirtle's face. Now that Squirtle could see, it aimed a

strong Skull Bash and won the round!

Solrock was Brandon's next Pokémon to enter the battle. Squirtle got trapped in Solrock's Confusion. Then, after a flash of Solar Beam, Squirtle was unable to battle.

Ash brought Bulbasaur back to the battlefield. It, too, got caught in Confusion and began to Vine Whip itself. Ash hugged his pal to try to protect it from hitting itself. With the support of his pal, Bulbasaur shook it off and went back on the attack. It tied up Solrock with Leech Seed and added a stunning Solar Beam. But Solrock fired a super Solar Beam right back. After the blasts, both Bulbasaur and Solrock were knocked out.

Now Ash and Brandon each had a single Pokémon left. Pikachu leaped onto the battlefield, ready to give its all! Brandon chose the large Legendary Ice-type Pokémon, Regice. Regice used Ice Beam to cover the field with ice. But Pikachu wasn't about to let anything stop it. It let out a Thunderbolt strike and a direct hit of Iron Tail.

Regice used Ice Beam to trap Pikachu behind frosty pillars. It slashed through the ice with Iron Tail. It raced toward Regice, but Regice trapped it in a block of Ice Beam. Pikachu was now frozen in a giant ice cube!

The referee began to call the match for Brandon when suddenly, a crack opened up in the ice, and a terrific Thunderbolt sprayed out of the cube! Pikachu was back on the battlefield and ready to heat things up!

Regice swung Focus Punch and made Pikachu bounce across the battlefield. Pikachu steadied itself and struck back-to-back wallops of Iron Tail. Regice trapped Pikachu in icy pillars again, but Pikachu sliced through the beams with Iron Tail, and raced toward Regice with Volt Tackle. Ash and Pikachu won the battle against Pyramid King Brandon—and Ash earned the title "Frontier Brain"!

Everyone gathered to congratulate Ash, including Brandon. Scott offered Ash the chance to have his own Battle Frontier. Ash thanked him for the generous offer, but said he still had too many places to go and people to meet. In short, Ash was ready for more adventure!

So, Ash bid good-bye to his dearest Pokémon pals. Bulbasaur went back to help Professor Oak at his lab. Squirtle rode off with Officer Jenny to rejoin his Squirtle Fire Squad. Charizard set off into the sunset, flying high.

And Ash, too, set back out on the road with Pikachu, ready for more fun! No matter where this Trainer goes, he brings all the lessons and the sweet memories he's shared with his first friends.